Life in a Forest

Written by Helen Mason
Illustrated by Chris Walker
Editor: Alan Ritchie

Copyright © 1992 by Helen Mason

All rights reserved. No part of this book may be reproduced or transmitted in any form or by any means, electronic or mechanical, including photocopying and recording, or by any information storage and retrieval system, without permission in writing from the publisher.

Durkin Hayes Publishing Ltd.
3312 Mainway, Burlington, Ontario L7M 1A7
One Colomba Drive, Niagara Falls, New York 14305

The **sloth** is at home in the treetops. Other smaller animals are at home on the sloth! Up to nine different kinds of moth can live in its fur. So can four kinds of beetles, six ticks and seven mites.

The sloth is even a home for plants! During the rainy season, green algae grow on its fur, making the sloth hard to see among the leaves.

You may have heard an owl hooting. But have you ever heard one flying? The silent flight of this **brown owl** will give no warning to the mouse it has spied scurrying along the ground.

What is a Forest?

Have you ever heard the expression, "You can't see the forest for the trees?" Standing in the middle of a silent forest, you might believe that the forest is nothing but trees. Don't believe it! There's a lot more to see if you stop, look, and listen.

People are so noisy! Forest creatures hear us coming and fall silent. Stop moving and listen. Sit quietly and wait. You'll soon discover that the forest is far more than just trees. It is a whole little world of birds and animals, plants and insects. Indeed, you may soon be wishing for bug repellent to get rid of some more annoying forest critters. Slap!

Perhaps a squirrel will scamper up a tree right in front of your eyes. But few forest creatures live at the height of your eyes. So look high above your head and search down on the ground. Some animals, like the squirrel, live high in the treetops. Others live on the forest floor. Many forest animals even live underground.

A **deer** finds plenty to eat in the forest— twigs, bark, grass and shoots. The early bird catches the deer. If you want to see one of these shy creatures, your best bet is to look in fields near the forest just after sunrise.

Shelf fungus grows on the side of a tree. Why do you think it has this name?

A sudden sharp whistle may make you jump. Maybe you've disturbed a groundhog or a chattering **chipmunk**. You may get a glimpse of them before they disappear. Where do they go? Both of these animals live in cosy burrows underground.

Life in the treetops is hard to explore. But you can find many fascinating creatures under rocks and logs on the forest floor. Many **salamanders** stay underground until the forest ground is wet. They eat insects, worms, snails and other small animals.

Life in a Deciduous Forest

Do you live near a deciduous forest? Here's a hint: 'deciduous' means 'to fall off.' Guess what falls off deciduous trees!

The leaves of deciduous trees change, following the seasons of the year.

Winter:
From late fall through early spring, the deciduous forest seems dead. There are no leaves on the branches. Snow may cover the ground. The forest isn't dead. It is only hibernating. Warm temperatures will bring back the plants and many of the animals.

Spring:
In the spring, the whole deciduous forest bursts with life. Spring is the season for wild flowers. Soon, new leaves are growing on the tree branches. They block out more and more sunlight. What happens to the wildflowers when leaves block their sun?

fox

rabbit

Life in a forest may be hidden right under your nose. That scaly stuff on rocks, for example. It's called **lichen**. Lichen is a combination of two different plants: **alga** and **fungus**. The alga makes food for the fungus. The fungus protects and stores water for the alga. Lichens are eaten by animals like caribou, deer and elk.

The forest floor is covered with a lot of dead plant material. This is called **leaf litter**.

Beneath the surface litter lies a thick layer of **humus**, built up over thousands of years. Humus is a rich food supply for plants in the forest.

painted trillium

Summer:

Most of us think of summer as a sunny season. In deciduous forests, summer is the gloomiest season. The umbrella of tree leaves means that few plants can grow on the forest floor.

Autumn:

Each autumn, tree leaves change to colors of brilliant red, yellow and orange. Then they die and fall to the ground. How many different kinds of leaves can you find? Preserve them by pressing them between pages of a book. You can also make a bright leaf bouquet.

In the fall, you may be surprised to find many different kinds of toadstools growing on the forest floor. Look but don't touch. Toadstools can be very poisonous. Even experts wash their hands after handling toadstools.

Do you know? Whether that plant you just picked is good to eat?

Here's a golden rule for any plant— leaf, berry or toadstool. Treat everything as if it is **deadly poison** until somebody who knows tells you different! Even then, let **them** eat it for lunch. You can try it yourself the next day if they haven't fallen ill. That way, you'll never make a mistake.

Better still, why pick plants at all? Instead, follow this naturalist's code. Take nothing but sketches and photographs Leave nothing but footprints.

Look closely around a rotting stump. You'll see animals that help to make forest soil. What are they doing to help? Be careful not to put your hand into any holes!

termite

pill bug

centipede

Life in a Coniferous Forest

Although coniferous trees are found in many climates, some kinds stand cold weather well. Their leaves have a special anti-freeze so that the food can still move through the tree. Where might you expect to find these hardy evergreens?

One easy answer: in the far north and south. Sure enough, the world's more northerly and southerly forests are coniferous. What's another chilly place to look for evergreens? Study this page for a clue to the answer.

A thick, waxy coating helps coniferous needles hold water. Try to scrape some wax off a needle and have a closer look.

Coniferous leaves are little spikes called needles. Most coniferous trees never lose their leaves. That's why we often call them 'evergreens.'

Coniferous trees sometimes grow all topsy turvy, especially in wet places. Conifers have shallow roots, which don't anchor them as well as many deciduous trees. Water-logged ground, frost and high winds all work together and tip trees to crazy angles.

Often there are not many other plants growing on the forest floor—even in the spring. The needles make a soft, spongy carpet, but they have a lot of acid in them. When they rot, they make a poor soil.

There is another good reason why there are fewer plants in an evergreen forest. Since the needles don't fall, the forest floor is often dark all year round, too dark for most plants to grow.

Just because there are fewer plants in a coniferous forest, don't give up exploring! The ones you find may well be worth the search!

Sundews, for example, have sweet-smelling, sticky leaves that attract and trap insects. They eat bugs because they cannot get the food they need from the poor soil.

sundew

Investigate:

The word 'coniferous' comes from the word 'cone.' You don't have to live near a forest to find conifer cones. How many different kinds can you find in your neighborhood? What are cones for?

Half-hidden on each cone is the same beautiful pattern. Can you find it?

The tallest trees in a tropical rain forest are higher than a fifteen-story building! The treetops grow so close together that little sunlight gets through to the floor of the forest.

Drip, drip, water falls from trees. It may be the only movement you see as you walk through a tropical rain forest.

But, high up in the penthouse, living things are everywhere! Many plants and animals make their homes where they can get some sunlight. They live so high above the forest floor that people have a very hard time studying them. Can you imagine climbing a fifteen-story ladder just to watch animals?

Orchids cling to the bark on trees. The roots of these orchids take food from the air instead of the soil as most plants do.

Vines twine around the trees. Their roots are in the ground, but their leaves and flowers are in the treetops.

The **strangle fig** starts to grow high in the branches of a tree, then sends its roots down to the forest floor. When the host tree dies, it is replaced by a fig tree.

If very little light reaches the forest floor, does it matter to plants?

Investigate:

Ask permission to block sunlight from the leaf of a house plant. Use tinfoil to make a little tent around the leaf. Make sure the leaf can get air. What happens to the leaf after a few weeks? Is sunlight necessary for it?

Some tropical forest animals, like the **ring-tailed lemur**, are active after dark when the temperature is cooler.

Many creatures in the rain forest are hardly ever seen by people. They live, hunt and die in the treetops. Some are well camouflaged, like the **green mamba snake**.

The Tropical Rain Forest

Tropical forests are hot. Many are also wet. These hot, wet forests are called **rain forests**. Rain forests can be very unpleasant places for humans to visit. But many, many kinds of plants and animals call these forests home.

In fact, of all the different kinds of plants and animals in the world, more than half live in tropical forests. Thousands of them have not yet been discovered.

Unfortunately, many tropical plants and animals will **never** be discovered. We are cutting down tropical forests so fast that some will become extinct before we even know about them!

Because of the heat and moisture, things decay quickly in a tropical forest. There is only a thin layer of plant and animal material rotting on the forest floor.

As in other forests, the tropical forest floor hides many kinds of life. Some of them can be dangerous! The **tarantula** lives in an underground burrow lined with silk.

Farm Forests

Did you eat anything today that came from a tree? In the supermarket, try to separate tree fruits from ones that grow on vines or bushes.

If you had an orange, grapefruit, apple, peach or pear, then you ate something from a forest. It didn't come from just any forest. Many of the fruits we eat come from 'orchards.' Orchards are special forests made by people.

Farmers carefully choose and plant orchard trees. They choose varieties that will grow best in the area they are farming. The trees are trimmed as they grow. If a tree dies, it is quickly removed and replaced.

Orchards grow more than fruit. Some nuts, such as pecans, pistachios, almonds and walnuts, grow in orchards. Other nuts, such as Brazil nuts, grow wild in tropical rain forests.

Coniferous trees also grow in orchards. This kind of orchard is usually called a tree farm. Each December, families arrive to choose and cut their own Christmas tree. You could call that a fruitful outing!

Investigate:

Visit an orchard. How is it different from a natural forest? Are there more of fewer kinds of trees in it? What do you notice about their heights or shapes? Are the trees arranged neatly or not? Are there other kinds of plants growing among the trees? Why do you think the trees are arranged and trimmed the way they are?

Investigate:

Next time you eat an apple or an orange, cut the fruit across. Take a close look at the cross-section. Do you see any pattern? What other fruits have a similar pattern?

Study the seeds carefully. How many are there? What size are they? What shape?

Make a collection of seeds. Is there a difference between the way seeds are designed? Can you begin to classify fruits according to the type of seeds they have? Do fruits with similar seeds also have similar cross-sections?

Take a close look at some nuts. Compare the seeds inside and the shells outside to the seeds and 'shells' of a fruit. Can you tell what fruit almonds are related to? That's a nutty question with a peachy answer!

Now look at the fruit and seed from the tree's point of view. Why do trees have fruits? Are they just producing a nice tasty snack? Or do people and animals help trees by eating their fruits?

Bees are farmers' friends. As bees move from blossom to blossom in search of nectar pollen, they carry pollen from flower to flower. Without pollen, trees won't grow fruit. Trees and bees have a BEE-utiful relationship. That's why many fruit farmers keep beehives in their orchards.

Managing nature isn't easy. People have made many mistakes learning how to produce food from forests. In the past, we've killed pests that were not pests at all, but helpful animals. Yes, trees and animals need each other. It takes both bees and foxes to make fruit. Odd but true!

ople farmers used to kill wolves and foxes until they oticed that there were more mice damaging the ees. Many farmers now let foxes and wolves stay nd hunt. They are natural mousetraps.

Breaking Down

Go for a walk in a damp forest. Decay is everywhere. You can smell it in the air. Is the forest dying?

Even though plants and animals are dying and decaying everywhere, the forest is very much alive.

In the forest, death and decay feed new life. Animals and plants eat each other, forming an endless **food chain**. Every link in this chain is precious. When people enter the forest and remove things, even a twig or a handful of dirt, we are removing a link in the chain.

Of course, some links (like a twig or even a whole tree) can be removed without endangering the forest. But if too many links in the chain are lost, the forest will die.

Mushrooms and other kinds of fungus help the process of decay. Their long root systems help to break down wood and break up soil.

Investigate:

Mold is a tiny fungus. To see how it grows, dampen a slice of bread. Add some dust. Seal the bread in a pastic bag and leave it in a dark place.

The roots of plants break up the soil. So do the tunnels of animals, such as **moles** and **earthworms**. This lets air and water reach countless billions of important creatures that need them. Can you see these creatures? Don't strain your eyes. They're the microscopic bacteria and other tiny plants and animals that cause decay. When they've finished their work, things that were once living are nothing more than chemicals. But those chemicals are important! They are the building blocks of all life, including yours.

Building Up

The forest breaks things down. Then it joins the bits and pieces to build new food. Building begins in the green leaves of the forest.

Decay has left important building-block chemicals in the soil. These are pulled in by tree and plant roots, then carried up to the leaves. The energy of the sun links those chemicals with others from air and water to make plant food. This process is called **photosynthesis**.

Bark beetles cut tunnels through tree bark. Disease and decay-causing creatures can enter through these holes.

How about a tasty bite of wood? Termites enjoy it, even if you don't. Like us, they can't digest their food without help. We have bacteria living in our digestive tract which help break down our food. Termites also need the help of bacteria, but ones which break down wood fiber instead!

This log is rotten. A **skunk** rips it open, looking for grubs and termite larvae. In the same way, people break down life in the forest. You might rip open a rotting log as you hunt for salamanders.

Is the skunk doing a good thing, while you do a bad one? Does the skunk help the forest while you hurt it? These are difficult questions to answer. They are worth a lot of thought.

Who Eats Whom?

Food chains can take many unusual twists and turns.

Here's a challenge. The animals below feed on each other. They can be arranged in a food chain. Put them in order.

If you get stuck, there's an explanation on page 32.

13

Forest Friends

Each member of the forest community has a special job to do. This is nature's way of protecting the forest.

The vulture is a large bird that acts as the forest's clean-up crew. It eats dead animals from the forest floor. Even if it doesn't live in the forest, the vulture is a constant visitor. With its keen eyesight, the vulture may be only a pinprick in the sky and yet it will still see a dead or dying animal. Next time you see a vulture high in the sky, squint at it. Can you tell how healthy it is? The vulture has probably seen you and already knows you're too healthy to be its next meal.

Tent caterpillars munch on tree leaves. If they eat too many tree leaves, the trees will die. People can kill the caterpillars with insecticides. But many insecticides can kill helpful insects, too.

Luckily, forests have their own non-human friends which help to maintain a healthy balance.

For example, there is a fly that helps keep caterpillars in balance. The fly lays its eggs on the caterpillar. The fly larvae eat the caterpillar before it can lay more eggs.

We all know that spiders are scary and flies are dirty and mice are cute and mosquitos are bad and honey bees are good.

These ideas may make sense for people, but not for the forest. Try to leave your own likes and dislikes behind as you explore nature!

A friend of the forest may have eight legs and live in a web, whether you like it or not!

Take the cap off an acorn. Break open a walnut. Split a berry. Inside you may find a grub or an insect tunnel. A plant seed has been destroyed by a little critter. These critters must be **enemies** of the forest, not friends, right?

Wrong! Trees produce billions of seeds. If every one grew into a tree, we would all live in a deep, dark forest.

The true friend of the forest is **balance.** A healthy balance between trees and animals comes with the help of all kinds of creepy, crawly, sticky, slimy critters. They, too, are friends of the forest.

Investigate:

How are seeds spread around the forest? If you don't live near a forest, collect lots of different seeds from trees and in your neighborhood. Stand on a chair and throw them up into the air. Which ones float away? Which ones spiral to the ground? What other ways do seeds move?

Think about squirrels and what they do with acorns. And what happens to the seeds in berries that are eaten by birds and bears?

Woodpeckers protect trees from damage by eating grubs and other insects living under the bark.

Did you know? Burrs are unbearable, even for a bear! But they're more than a useless nuisance. Burrs are clever little seed pods taking a free ride on your sweater!

Hummingbirds, bees and butterflies sip nectar from blossoms. As they do so, they move pollen from one flower to another. Some blossoms need pollen from other blossoms in order to make seeds.

Life Among the Branches

Could you live high in the branches of a tree? Probably not. As soon as you fell asleep, you would fall out. But some animals spend most of their lives in trees. Their bodies are built in ways that help them use trees. These ways are called **adaptations**.

tree frog

On these pages are several animals that can be found in the treetops. Can you match them with the descriptions that follow? Check your answers on page 32.

1. I have short legs with four toes. Two of my toes point forward, two backward. This helps me to climb. I can prop my stiff tail against the tree trunk for balance.

2. I have small, sticky pads on my feet. These help me to climb straight up the trunk of a tree.

3. The tip of my tail has a never-slip grip. This helps me swing through tree branches.

4. I have a beak like a needle which I use to sew leaves together to make my nest.

5. I don't live in a tree, but I'm really high on them! I eat tree leaves and my body is designed to reach them. You won't find me in the deepest forests, but I love to browse in open woodlands.

6. I can spread out my ribs like Superman's cape. This works like a parachute when I move from branch to branch.

downy woodpecker

Investigate:
Do animals that live on the ground move differently from those that live in trees? Budgies and canaries normally live in trees. A cat visits treetops. How often do you see dogs climbing trees?

Compare the feet and limbs of these three animals. What special **adaptations** do they have for their kind of life?

17

Funny Forest Shapes

Have you ever seen a tree with a strange shape and wondered how it grew that way? Natural forces can make trees grow in funny ways.

Sometimes a new tree will grow on the stump of a dead one. When the stump finally rots away, it leaves the new tree looking as if it is standing on its fingers.

Trees growing along the seashore are sprayed by saltwater. Salt harms the buds and leaves on the side facing the water. The tree looks lopsided. The same thing can happen along forest roads that are salted in winter.

Investigate:

1. Put a sprouting potato in some soil in a pot.
2. Cut a hole in one end of a shoebox.
3. Place the pot in the other end of the shoebox.
4. Tape cardboard strips between the pot and the hole.
5. Close the lid. Remove it only to water potato.
6. In a few weeks, what happens?

Keep your eyes open for strangely shaped tree trunks. Sometimes a disease twists them; sometimes lightning or high winds. If you accidentally step on a young tree, it may grow with a bend or twist in it.

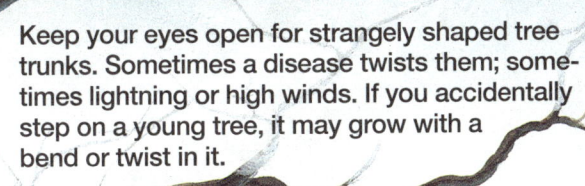

A Tree Surprise

One day a farmer hung a horseshoe on a tree. Many years later some woodcutters were cutting down that tree when their saw hit metal. The tree had kept on growing and grew right over the horseshoe!

In the same way, wire fencing that is nailed to a tree often winds up buried inside it. A surprise with a handsaw can be a disaster with a modern chain saw. When a chain saw hits metal in a tree, it can jerk back and injure or kill the lumberjack.

In recent years, people have tried to prevent forests from being cut down. They have threatened to put spikes into trees so that lumberjacks will be afraid to cut them! Some people feel very strongly about preserving our forests!

Investigate:

As a new tree searches for sunlight in a crowded forest, it will often grow at an angle. To see how this happens, try placing a plant in a sunny window for a week. Look where the leaves are. Turn the plant around and watch how the leaves bend to face the sun.

Forest Champions

Palm trees are the skinniest of the big trees. They stay thin as they grow taller, unlike other kinds of trees.

The **macrozamia** has the world's largest cones. They weigh up to forty kilograms (eighty-eight pounds).

The **Seychelles palm** grows the world's largest nuts. They would probably be too wide to fit through your bedroom doorway. Imagine the size of the squirrel that could bury one!

Imagine hanging an eighty pound pine cone on a Christmas tree!

Douglas fir bark

Douglas fir tree bark can grow almost as thick as your school desk is wide.

palm nut

Baobab trees are the fattest. They can be twelve meters (thirteen yards) around.

baobab

They are so so big that an Australian town made a baobab tree into a jail.

Seychelles palm

Investigate:

How can you tell one tree from another? It will help to bring a field guide to trees into the forest.

What do you need to identify a tree?

1) One or more leaves. Leaf shape is a big clue to the type of tree.

2) Twigs. The pattern of leaves on a branch is sometimes important.

3) Bark. It sometimes looks different on young and old trees.

4) Seeds or blossoms, if you can find any.

Ordinary and Extraordinary

It's always exciting to catch a glimpse of something unusual in the forest—a brightly colored salamander, a brilliant orange oriole, a red fox trotting down a path. But even as you keep your eyes peeled for special things, there's lots to explore right under your very nose. Trees, for example. How many kinds are there in your forest? It can be fun to try and answer that question.

The **jumping mouse** weighs less than a handful of crackers. Yet in one leap it can jump three meters (nine feet) high! If you were just as strong for your own weight, you'd be able to jump six kilometers (four miles) high!

Two Unusual Forest High-Fliers

No, these high-fliers are not birds as you might expect, but the **jumping mouse** and the **gray fox!**

The **gray fox** is a member of the dog family. Everybody knows that dogs don't climb trees, but somebody forgot to tell the gray fox! It will even sleep up in a bushy tree from time to time.

Interesting Forest Facts

The World's Tallest Tree

The California redwood tree lives today and the brachiosaurus dinosaur lived millions of years ago. They both hold height records for living things. You would have to walk up four flights of stairs to reach the head of the huge dinosaur. You'd have to walk up forty flights to reach the top of a California redwood!

Counting Birthdays

Do you know how to tell the age of a tree? Most years, a tree grows a new layer of wood. You can more or less tell the age of a tree by counting the dark rings in the trunk — each ring roughly stands for one year of the tree's life. How old is the tree below?

Why do Leaves Change Color?

Leaves are green because of a natural ingredient called **chlorophyll.** Chlorophyll helps the leaves make food energy from sunlight. In the fall, as the hours of sunlight grow shorter, the chlorophyll stops working. The bright green color fades, allowing other colors to appear. That's when we see the beautiful red, orange and yellow leaves of autumn.

Why do Trees Pop?

If you wear a ring, you know what happens to your fingers on a very cold day. In the same way, the bark of a tree shrinks in the cold. It can shrink so much that it no longer fits the tree trunk, like a shirt sleeve that's too tight. Then you'll hear the bark split with a loud popping noise.

A Forest Frozen in Time

Have you ever seen a tree millions of years old? They're not that rare! The trees are dead, of course, but they're still around. Some time after they died, these prehistoric trees became soaked with water containing a mineral called silica, which turned them into a fossil we call **petrified wood.**

Treasures from Trees

Over thousands of years, people have learned to harvest many wonderful crops from trees. Nearly everybody knows the two most important.

Without moving from the room, how many things can you see around you that are made of wood from trees?

There are many other important things that come from trees.

Can you match four different trees with the things that grow on them? Find the answers on page 32.

1. My seeds, or beans, were once used as money in South America. An explorer named Cortez brought some of them to Europe more than four hundred years ago. Today, the seeds are used to make a treat that is loved all over the world.

2. In the spring, people collect my sap and boil it into a sweet syrup. I am found only in eastern North America. Indians first learned how to use my sap.

3. The juice from my berries is used in rat poison and in the plots of many murder mysteries. Other trees in my family were once used to make poison to tip arrows and blowguns. I'm sometimes injected as a drug after people suffer a heart attack or a drug overdose.

4. Many people used to think that I could chase away bad spirits. They made brooms out of my wood because they thought they could sweep bad things out of their houses. I was also used to make canes for beating the badness out of children!

strychnos nux vomica tree

white birch

Forest Camouflage

When we are in danger, most of us would rather hide than stand out in a crowd. Many creatures in the forest survive by hiding. They **camouflage** themselves so they are hard to see.

Look carefully at the bottom of this page. That's not just a collection of twigs, but a **walking stick insect**, pretending to be part of the tree. What would you wear to camouflage yourself in the woods?

There are times when it is much safer to stand out so that you are easily noticed. During hunting season in the fall, be sure you are wearing bright yellows, reds and orange colors if you walk in the woods. Or be even smarter and become completely invisible. Don't go into forests at all during hunting season!

cacao tree

sugar maple

walnut tree

Trees produce treasures for themselves first and not for us. The black walnut, for example, produces a kind of chemical that stops other plants from growing nearby. That's not much use to people, but can you think of how it might help the walnut tree?

The Two Sides of Fire

Forest fires, whether started by lightning or by people, destroy much of the life in a forest. Millions of hectares (acres) of forest are burned each year. The fires kill many of the living things in the forest.

Occasional forest fires can be helpful to the forest. They kill taller, older trees, and clear land for new trees to grow. Some plants and animals actually depend on forest fires.

The **jack pine** grows best after fires have cleared the area. The heat of the fire releases the jack pine's seeds from its cones. The seedlings sprout in the sunlight and open space left after the fire.

Investigate:

Do you know what kinds of things start forest fires? Do you know what to do to prevent them? To find out, visit your local fire station or conservation area.

Before people began to play with fire, occasional forest fires, tens or even hundreds of years apart, helped keep a forest healthy. But too many fires are a disaster for the forest plants and animals.

Don't forget, we need the forests in order to harvest wood and other crops. So too many forest fires are disastrous for us as well.

People start more forest fires than lightning. But lightning fires often do more damage. That's because human carelessness usually starts fires nearer roads. It's harder to fight a fire started by lightning far off in the wilderness.

jack pine cones

Kirtland's warblers need forest fires. They build their nests on the ground beneath young jack pine trees. If there are no fires, pine cones will not open to release their seeds. If there are no young jack pines, there are no Kirtland's warblers.

Endangered Forests

All over the world forests are being destroyed to make room for towns, farms, hydro dams, roads and mines. Some forests are also being killed by pollution.

Cutting down forests can make deserts. Many forest soils are very poor. They have barely enough food in them to support the forest. Everything that dies in the forest **must** become food for more plants, or the forest itself will die. So what happens if we take all the trees away? The soil grows poorer. It can no longer support new plants.

Without plants, what happens to the soil then? Here's an interesting summertime experiment. Point a garden hose at your lawn. What happens to the dirt under the grass? Anything?

Now point the hose at bare dirt. What happens?

Trees and plants "anchor" the soil. Without an anchor, soil washes away in the rain. This is called **soil erosion**. What was once a forest becomes a desert of ditches and gullies.

How can we help to save our forests? Many things we use in our lives come from trees. If we can use less, we can help save forests.

Don't be wasteful. Practice "the three Rs": Reduce, Reuse, Recycle. If you don't need it, don't take it. If it's still good, use it again or find another use for it. Why not see if you can find a new use for something that you were going to throw out today?

As forests disappear, so do many plants, animals and birds. If a living thing is in danger of dying out completely, then it is an **endangered species**.

Every year more and more species join the list.

The bald eagle, the peregrine falcon, the eastern cougar, the Asiatic elephant and the diamondback rattlesnake are just a few of the endangered species that need our protection. What can you do to help them?

Be a Forester

Elzeard Bouffier was a shepherd who lived in a desert region of France. Between 1910 and 1947, he planted thousands of oak, linden, beech, birch and maple trees.

These trees improved the land. Their roots dug into the soil and helped to keep water in the ground. Streams that had gone dry began to flow again. The land became beautiful. More than ten thousand people came to make their homes there, all because one person cared enough to plant trees.

Get involved in tree-planting projects in your neighborhood. Collect money to help protect an acre of rain forest, or to plant trees in the African desert. Even though you may not live in the rain forest or the desert, you need trees there, too. Forests around the world purify air that all of us breathe. Without those forests we will all be in serious trouble!

Investigate:

Take the temperature under a tree on a hot day. Take a second temperature out in the open. Is there a difference?

To find out why, tie a clear plastic bag around a large tree leaf that has hot sunlight falling on it. Leave it for twenty minutes. What appears on the inside of the bag?

When you sweat, water appears on your skin. When the water evaporates, your skin is cooled. In the same way, leaves and plants 'air condition' the forest.

Grow an Avocado Tree

1. Fill a small glass with water.

2. Carefully peel the brown covering from an avocado pit. Insert toothpicks into the seed.

3. Suspend the seed in the glass. Keep the glass filled with water.

4. When the stem and roots have grown about the height of your hand, remove the seed from the water. Remove the toothpicks.

5. Fill a flowerpot with soil. Now plant your tree.

What other kinds of trees can you grow?

Experiment with the seeds of oranges, limes, grapefruits or lemons. Take the largest seeds from the fruit and keep them in water until you are ready to plant. Place them in a flowerpot filled with soil and cover with a centimeter of soil. Keep in a sunny spot and add enough water to keep the soil damp.

Answers for page 13

At the bottom of this food chain is the **deer**.

The **female mosquito** drinks the blood of the deer.

The **dragonfly** eats the mosquito.

The next two animals can be in either order at the top of the food chain!

Both the **bat** and the **frog** will eat a dragonfly.

Believe it or not, there are bats that eat frogs, and frogs that eat bats!

Answers for pages 16-17

1. Downy woodpecker
2. Tree frog
3. Spider monkey
4. Tailorbird
5. Giraffe
6. Flying dragon

Answers for pages 24-25

1. Cacao tree, used for making chocolate.
2. Sugar maple tree, used for making maple syrup.
3. Strychnos Nux vomica tree, used for making strychnine, a poison and a drug.
4. White birch tree, used to make brooms to sweep out evil spirits.